ARCHICEMBALO

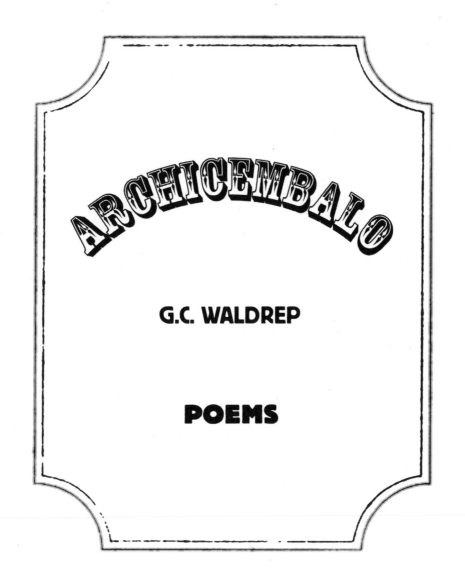

ARCHICEMBALO

G.C. WALDREP

POEMS

T P

TUPELO PRESS

North Adams, Massachusetts

Achicembalo Copyright © 2009 G.C. Waldrep
ISBN: 978-1-932195-74-3
LCCN: 2008907826

First paperback edition April 2009

Tupelo Press, Inc.
PO Box 1767
Eclipse Mill, 243 Union Street, Loft 305
North Adams, Massachusetts 01247
Telephone: 413-664-9611 / Fax: 413-664-9711
editor@tupelopress.org / tupelopress.org

Cover and text designed by William Kuch, WK Graphic Design

Tupelo Press is an award-winning independent literary press
that publishes fine fiction, non-fiction and poetry in books that are as
much a joy to hold as they are to read.

Tupelo Press is a registered 501(c)3 non-profit organization and relies on
donations to carry out its mission of publishing extraordinary work that
may be outside the realm of the large commercial publisher.

Supported in part by an award from the
National Endowment for the Arts

NATIONAL
ENDOWMENT
FOR THE ARTS

for Jameson Marvin

TABLE of CONTENTS

"Who is Josquin des Prez".. 1

"What is a Hymn".. 3

"What is Selah" (I)... 4

"What is an Anthem"... 5

"What is a Fugue" 7

"What is a Mordent".. 7

"What is an Overtone" 7

"What is a Zither" 8

"What is a Gimel".. 9

"Who is Charles Ives".. 10

"What is an Antiphon"... 11

"What is Cadence" (II)... 13

"What is Opera"... 15

"Who was Scheherazade"... 21

"What is Serialism"... 23

"What is a Key Signature"... 23

"What is a Tenor" 23

"What is a Tritone.. 24

"What is a Hexachord" 26

"What is a Piano"... 28

"What is the Real Answer".. 29

"What is Pulse" 31

"What is Sforzando" 33

"What is a Soprano" 34

"What is an Arpeggio"... 35

"What is a Bass".. 37

"What is a Cantilena" 38

"What is Counterpoint"..40

"What is a Descant"...40

"Who is Johannes Ockegehm".......................................41

"What is Cadence" (I) 42

"Who is Anton Webern"..43

"What is a Cittern" 45

"Who is Friedrich von Schiller"....................................47

"What is an Arpanetta"...49

"What is Ictus"...50

"What is a Ballet" 50

"What is an Alto" 50

"What is Selah" (II) 50

"What is a Hornpipe" 51

"What is the Brotherhood" 52

"Apostrophe to the Memory of Benjamin Britten" 54

"What is Radio" 55

"What is a Canzone"..57

"What is a Hemiola"..57

:What is a Motet 58

"What is a Ballad"..58

"What is a Threnody" 59

"Who is Thelonious Monk"...60

"Who is Steve Reich" 60

"What is an Oratorio" 60

"What is Acciaccatura" 60

"Who were the Lorelei" 61

"What is a Metaphor"...62

"What is Performance"..63

"What is a Testimony" 64

Note 66

Acknowledgments 68

Accomplished students of happiness and experts in the full range of pleasure and joy—what leads us now to acknowledge another kind of learning in us, an understanding to which there remain deep inside us an indefinite number of witnesses?
—Pascal Quignard

WHO IS JOSQUIN DES PREZ

A little winter, a drop at winter, a descent and then a steeper dwindling in the depths of winter, a snowdrop. A small sketch. A snowdrop signals the end of one thing and the beginning of another, a wider imprecation. How do you do. How does one do. A snowdrop reminds.

To begin. There is a market, there is buying and selling, there is that proverbial marrying and being given in marriage as one joins another. And suits this action, as from field, as from the space defined within a field, as from a white flag. Sixteen cents allowing for the anachronism which is a necessary liberty as with marriage as with may I hold you, may I kiss your lips, may I move my hand between your cheek and neck, between your neck and the basin of your shoulders. May I purchase this felt hat. Yes thank you.

In the road they were married and marrying. In the mud and dung which were frozen it being winter, or almost winter, or barely yet winter signaling outward to some different season. Some on horseback, some on foot. They were not thinking of dying. They were trading places with the dead, this is continual, this from moment to moment is what we call life. Some were some were not thinking of money. Some were not thinking of sleep.

What is sleep. Sleep is the penetration of value by a perfect means.

In any resurrection there may be doubts, there may be misgivings, there may well be interruptions, there may be the confidence of a period style. There may be distortion this may be one aim. Any performance is a rondeau and so not drawn from legacy. Any performance is provisional, as pence for francs or dollars for rubles. (See *What is ballet.*)

1

If one cannot imagine a snowdrop then one might imagine its absence. A snowdrop as its own absence, a snowdrop is its own absence, a snowdrop absent. A snowdrop. White on white / on white.

WHAT IS A HYMN

A vault kneeling stresses rhythm from one frozen motion. This is not about time. This is not about the consideration of another's feelings. Another may come or go, may come and go, another may come or she may go and he may come again. This is not about personality. Whereas from a lectern any ice needle threads broadcloth some sure vacancy.

Another may come or go, another may come or he may go and may not come again. If the other is yoked, if the other is tired, if the other is frightened. If the other is very small. And so how round a vowel is it that forces static from the elms into a pale sky. We see this as candles.

The question is not which but another in his freedom, that is, in the expression of a broader interest or concern, excitement or distaste. Call it nave or gable or something yet more curious eggs pelican cheese.

A cantonment for one certain culture.

Threshold then is not the same as permission, i.e. may he come, may she go, may another substitute—reluctant creel—may *there* prick an absence, may I be alone. I am alone and want and therefore you too with me. Purely voluntary. Or not at all voluntary else not pure. Is there any strength in the mutual application of a fixed surface.

Is not then paper, is not then voice. Drawn down from scope to hand-held satisfaction the plane of a dubious embrace. I question as does each in its small way. When thrown to the harp as eggs, as pelican, as license, as cheese it makes a simple roaming, it splays tethered, it does not go far. It can be heard across the river. It is an obstruction in a winter park.

What is red, a hymn is a red dress, a hymn is a red dress that keeps swinging.

3

WHAT IS SELAH (I)

A city inside keeps crumbling into dust.

Nothing in particular is wrong, nothing in particular is a gradual unfolding and thereby undaunted by underlying technique, this is an aesthetic reproach, a taunt, a distinction and an astonishment. Space makes weight and way for malingering artifice, for a vision touching the whole multitude thereof.

Any mock-up of the universe depends on touch for its root semblance. Is there, was there ever a demiurge. (See *What is architecture.*)

Every native with his destroying weapon looks past one wheel into another. Every David in the stateroom of his agony asks for an interpretive sign: is it better not to know, is this a Hebrew letter, is this an Etruscan conceit. Translucent. In which dimension hubris manifests and whereby renewed through what polarity.

A sympathy, as for cherish. A stilled dancing in the fens of the Brooklyns.

A vantage in the valley of dry bones. (Far ahead, an old woman paces the same road before you.)

WHAT IS AN ANTHEM

I sought a near care and left without having paid any particular price, I was not stingy, I did not think I was covetous, perhaps I betrayed a more vivid avulsion but I was not without integrity, I was possessed of a certain bodily charm.

When a charm grows ghoulish it demands more from the body, it is a consumptive delight.

I left the money on the table. Each penny separate and together, this is copper, this is how copper behaves: most elegant at high noon burnish. Like noon a furnished room requests the pleasure of a body's judgment, its sovereign will, as seen in the shadow a hinged door makes, as seen in a cannon's mouth.

What is inheritance, inheritance is subjugation of time through flesh, it is a staying motion and like a harp's pedal but more slowly, it remains an intervailing conceit. I left the money on the table, I made every calculation.

Is this pretty at a distance.

When one is beautiful (which is to say when one has inherited) one may stand alone. Does this make one lonely, does this make one less beautiful or more, does this express a miserly disposition and if so when and to what purpose.

The country around Karbala is desert, meaning a dry wind and sand and pilgrims in like season, later skirmish coached with salt. What is a desert, a desert *is*, an empty desert makes one beautiful, an emptied desert is a breach and thus makes also whole.

I was walking away but I had left the money on the table. This is a question of citizenship, this cannot be disputed. I was not giving up anything, I was within my rights, I was perfectly assured.

I left the money on the table and walked down to the bridge.

A bridge asks more of us. A bridge asks for commitment, a bridge is the instrument of a plaintive investiture, a bridge is the negation of one reputable stance. A bridge is an argument about form, a toll. A bridge may be a disguise.

To be alone one must be beautiful. To be beautiful one must be alone. To lie, with her and again precludes the possibility, to speak when spoken to is a modified circumspection.

To look into a cannon's mouth is likewise an argument about solitude, it is a risky business. Does this make one beautiful. Of course. Which we have done and more surely for not wanting enough, for not waiting, for wasting and not trusting and for so. *In my father's house are many mansions.* Does this absolve.

I left the money on the table and walked down to the bridge. Root and stone, my heart gives way to a third arm. I felt and I thought I was done.

WHAT IS A FUGUE

A good dog comes lightly, a good dog comes nightly is pet and is petted and in this way we know the faculty of exuberance. There is a bounding a stretching forth there is a limb and within the limb a letter and it is carried. And will it be consumed, pressed tin ceilings and the spaces for fans that perhaps once turned but are now fixed like nipples in rows and columns. This is the math of it. A good dog knows when to lie down.

WHAT IS A MORDENT

In the photos only the eyes of the horses were visible. Haymote in the dustmow; silk scavenger. Bladed gnomon of each Greek night.

WHAT IS AN OVERTONE

Skein of white wheat. A bright treat. No longer any need for windows in the palace. No longer any palace in the noonday sun.

WHAT IS A ZITHER

An all-but-unnoticed humming on the Island of the Uncommitted.

Is there some secret history I'm missing. The hokey-pokey, for instance. *Right foot in, left foot out; shake it all about.* St. Mary Murgatroyd. St. Mary Murgatroyd again. Would skiing be such a strenuous exercise if we were all very small.

I trace a continental divide, I confess a mapmaker's fetish, with my eighth finger I part that ocean. Stinking mudflats at dawn. I did not think to bring a theosophical treatise.

Have you any canned milk.

In its domestic form, an autoharp. A ball of yarn, a small dish of potpourri, a plaster figurine. This is my archaeological inquiry, this is the origin of a classical disposition. If you had a lifetime for boardgames which one would you sooner play.

WHAT IS A GIMEL

I call for song and paper answers, this is a physical act though practiced above the board of conspicuous consumption, though perfected in the wake of a pleasant repast. A quantity of linen risks no special disgrace.

Rules, what are rules, rules are discrete and affect the eye as does nutmeg, as does garlic, rules are *art brut*, rules are handsome, rules may suggest a Carthaginian exposure. At some depths a faith may be constructed. Rules are safe conduct, upward and how so.

A poet, a diplomat, and an interpreter walk into a bar. Is this funny, is this an aliquot part.

If I take your hand and you agree. If I take your hand do you agree. If I take your hand but you do not agree. If I take your hand, suddenly, if I take your hand, violently, if I take your hand, inviolately, if you are forced to act or not and for how long. At what point and in what sense does which motive hold. My boon companion. Could this be choice.

Does anger make one beautiful. Yes. Am I then angry. Yes.

If we stand together and watch two swans will we be changed. (See *What is harmony.*) I did not say improvise. And lightly but for perlustration of a generous bequest, a continental chalcography, I had hardly thought to present my relic, to scrape away the words, my countenance, to lay a dance track, to restore any former occasion or scalewise concern.

(There remains my recusancy, a small thing, nothing really, from English to French to German Italian and back again should I so playful choose—)

WHO IS CHARLES IVES

Assuming a body of water has depth there is also current, there is
historical affirmation of a raucous semblance, there is recession, there is
any hidden pact. A canvas votary. And the night fables. Each press of skin
patching narrative with its fresh lace.

Should we entertain. And if so eagerly. Riding down to Bangor have we any
occasion to suspect, have we given thought to bread, have we acknowledged
that tidal sacrament, have we forwarded a letter of introduction to the
proper authorities and have we requested secondly the pleasure of the
first, have we gleaned, have we averted, have we gravely set the silk of one
delirious intention among the rocks and cedars.

Pick a card. Pick two.

When a venue settles iron on a scale from six to eight is there any room
left for convention—such bagatelles!—for touch or for dense chatter.
And is so then and under what rich concern. When at last he heard did
he then measure. Can we verify the holograph.

(Though this is, this cannot, this must not be about money. Though this
will not be about night. Though this exists entirely within the sphere of
calculation. And must it. For without can magnificence yet abide.)

A wild teeming. As when a glance with reverence subtracts its lavish
raven. I walked, and found a warm breath there. One single plenty
is enough.

WHAT IS AN ANTIPHON

Ceiled in seven voices like a Scottish mass. Prolation of the inevitable. A small girl on a city square with a piece of chalk in her hand. Either she makes a mark with it or not.

Ceiled by train, ceiled by city, ceiled by square. A small girl in seven Scottish masses.

Egress by the train a small girl makes. The chalk is a cliff used for writing, a sort of balloon in which the souls of drowned boys wander. That drift, that illimitable wafting. The cliffs close around the landscape like a wound.

Either she makes a mark with it or not: chalk on skin, chalk on silk or gingham, chalk on flagstone. Chalk on bark, chalk on grass. Chalk on hair. Chalk perhaps on chalk.

Ceiled with egress, the inevitable glistening of the eyes. Clastic pinwheel sutra. From her bed in the round wound of the abbey a small girl dreams of her life in the balloon. She does not see the boys, who crowd toward and away from her, fearful, curious.

Each boy is a square city made of chalk. To sing in such a city is to pray to a distance.

She thinks this is a kind of freedom, ceiled with the most excellent train the balloon makes in the great cut-glass oracle of the sky. The inevitable intoxicant, mixed with bark & gall.

The train closes around the girl like a wound, like a high Scottish mass, like a bone bell. The skin of it a velvet chain across the pastures. The velvet is spun from the soft stomachs of bees. The bees drink from the cliffs inside of which boys keep drowning.

Thus: a belaying. No space through which laughter may exclude. There is a physical analogue to the absence of legend in landscape. Either the train makes a mark with her or not.

WHAT IS CADENCE (II)

Ask if this showing will make a better weave. Does one mistake a pig for a dog, a dog for a bear, a bear for a horse, does one mistake a horse for a pig though very small, does this disenfranchise, does it require a discrete referendum and if so how often and besides.

A prayer wheel resolves any broad theft: yes or no.

If I subtract sacrifice from appetite from what fierce attention do I then compromise a strict union, have I faltered, have I made an argument for grace. What is union, time's whistles and bells, the whole commodious diapason behind which a third nation lingers. In one variant you whisper *Sweet prince, sweet prince.* In another *I am the handmaid of the Lord.*

Into or out of can I buy my way, can I ply my way, by what prescribed motion does this egress take a spectral reading or from what distance do these colors run.

Do I yet withstand the adoption.

In a village in the Pyrenees snow is filed in the vaults of a decrepit museum. This is this is the archive of every chill and arctic blow. Shall I then take you, bundled in shed life and waiting. And what token will you bear, no coin of any pleasant realm will suffice, no calorie, no torrid receipt, the doorkeeper is my personal friend but he makes no exceptions, you must explain yourself, you must display the badge that I vouchsafe, that I cannot dispense, this is a complex admission, you must give satisfactory account.

Things happen while you sleep. Some of them happen to you.

I favor a candling essence. Can one learn from Plato (after all) or is "mixed" really just the imperfect in its most common form, does this require any special station or redress, is this a fraternal achievement.

Perfect: corm and nightblood. *Interrupted:* the central story. *Imperfect:* a master of this generation. *Plagal:* his iron wheel.

—My kerchief, my agon, my Easter, my bright gradient hum.

WHAT IS OPERA

Max Ernst, *La femme 100 têtes*

ACT I

Crime or miracle: a complete man. And drawn from the sky, what is the force of a dozen arms, two dozen, three, what is it to be *human*, what is the pallor that illuminates and which face, is it one among many, is this an immaculate retort.

I sing of arms and theft. A hoary office. You may hum along.

At the cove this morning I posted a thick letter, witness my germinal seed. A cotyledon distends the perfection of any discrete encounter, this is biology, a soothsayer's prognostication, this is a night visit and poses further questions, *viz.* does a shift in landscape preclude a tropical allusion, can we number the dependencies of any port town, can we perfume a monastic enclosure. Is this scholarship, is it gendered and how so. I look to the sea from whence cometh my kelp.

Stage direction: portrait and overture.

The sky opens twice. By what manipulation, by what updraft subtended does the divine reveal. If I play a distinctive chord may the children dawdle. May I join them, may the runners present themselves at the exterminal tape.

In the heart of Paris, Loplop, Bird-Superior, brings nightly food to the streetlamps. The unconsciousness of the parabola waxes complete.

ACT II

To tenderest youth, extreme unction. By what parallax do I enjoy this pleasant vocation, do I excurt and are we excused, is this what Eliot meant, *under the bam, under the boo, under the bamboo tree.* Have I grasped any Cartesian maxim. I should not have said so.

Stage direction: wires and harness. (See *What is Roman Catholicism.*)

The first touches of grace and unresolved games are being prepared here. Nothing is so detrimental as a competitive introspection, this can be proven, this is an aerobic fandango, can this be demonstrated precisely on green felt. Sweet chiliasm of the immoderately endowed.

How appropriate and appropriated then by whom and wherefore. Is this an illicit reproduction, by what limb then does this narrative hang, in what horoscope does the veil reside or have I merely exchanged transplendence for a negative exposure, was this intentional, should I leave you to guess and for how long, should you close your eyes, should you begin counting now.

Stage direction: lashed to a wind-swept spar.

ACT III

One sees more than hypethral devotion, this is a polyphony, a reprehensible descant, an infandous serenade. By what wick are we sighted and for how long.

(Consider translation. This is a recondite subject, this is a stupendous meringue. Does one paint. Does one telegraph. Does one compose, if given to waiting then does one cultivate any certain friendship, do I or does anyone bide my time. I exult in an expanded font, I rejoice in a prescripted likeness. I propose, may I propose a toast to the manufacturers of glass, may I break a pencil. Here, it is broken. Hurrah, we are many, we are whole again.)

Some favor a pointillist crusade. Did we meet them, did we convey any certain title, have they received any forbidden communique. Is it spring again already.

Stage direction: water sports.

With the third mouse seated, one sees the flying body of a legendary adult. I reject the pathetic fallacy. Loplop, a swallow, passes by.

ACT IV

I am casting a bronze for the last vestiges of public worship, that restless gibbet. I am a receptive disciple, I am the relict of St. Mary Murgatroyd. Have you read of her sanctity, her miracles, her incorruptible corpse. Her shoes were electrical, her ectype savage, her girdle an anabatic conceit. The samba you know is better than the bossanova you don't.

The sphinx and the daily bread visit this convent.

If one has not read a book, any book, will a picture suffice. Say, a sea epic. Say, *Moby-Dick*. Is there any such apparel. What if one prefers not to. I had not expected allegory. *Robespierre, Robespierre, wherefore art thou, Robespierre.*

Phenomenal and noumenal. Stage direction: municipal bonds.

Does one prefer company, does this compromise any unitary referral. Almost alone now with the ghosts and the ants I am certain you mimic a candle's selective reprise.

ENTR'ACTE

ACT V

The relationship between violence and freedom: explain. Is this an argument for reclusion, is this a Jungian archetype, is this a charitable analysis and at what *pro bono* rate. I ask merely to clarify. All around us images are descending, understand: this is no sweet spontaneous earth.

Does one carry the wounded. Emma Goldman will.

Max Ernst, who is Max Ernst, it is a pity Max Ernst never watched Patrick McGoohan in *The Prisoner* or perhaps he did, his was an invasion of correspondences, his was the flower of an infinite paranoia. Did he hold stock in which corporations and how much, did this qualify as sponsorship, was his a sweatshop aesthetic or was he just happy to see us.

Stage direction: a Swiss Alp.

Truth will remain simple, will discover the germ of very precious visions in the blindness of wheelwrights. Enter: the cartoon assassin, his cloak and dagger, her nitid comb.

ACT VI

A mythopoeic masque. If I say Mars do you say Saturn, if I say Anansi do you say Malathion, if I say Jehovah do you say Isuzu, if I say Cheops do you say wine.

Stage direction: dawn in the exploding restaurant. In the caves at Lascaux there is a pictograph that perfectly maps the West London theater district. Is this a foreshadowing, is this some cosmic joke. I slip a coin into the jukebox and get a racialized discourse, I get a book review, I did not press that button. (See *What is Pop.*)

Was he obsessed with laundry. Yes.

Night screams in her lair and approaches our eyes like raw flesh. One story about Peggy Guggenheim is as good as another.

If only I could walk away from this altar. Mind the footlights. Meanwhile the astigmatic are healed, the lame walk, my goofy neighbors speak in tongues. At his death Max Ernst's estate included sixteen kachinas, nine works by Native Americans of the northwest coast, twenty-eight from New Guinea and New Ireland, seven from Africa, and three from the Inuits.

I say Coyote, you say Cthulhu, let's call the whole thing off.

ACT VII

Aria: Pearl Buck. High time we reconsider, this is an exemplary convergence, let us encourage the graduate students, let us fund a festschrift, let us convene a symposium, let us marshal the dons. Let us terrace the rice fields, let us take advantage of the Dow. Tourists demand this of us and more.

All doors look alike. Encrypted any opus seems like so much white noise, this is usual, this is a primitive furnace, this is my royal flush.

In New York City the housing problem has caused all five boroughs to sell vertical space beneath the major bridges and access ramps. Is this different, building down rather than up, will the units be rent controlled, which will prove the most popular, is this my grave in the air. Would I lie to you.

Can one sleep suspended over water.

Aria: Pearl Buck.

Seduced by silence, a door opens backwards. *A body without a body lies down beside its bed and, like a phantom without a phantom, and with a special saliva, shows us the way to the womb.*

ACT VIII

Enter: the monkey who will be a policeman, a Catholic, a broker; Fantômas; Dante and Jules Verne; Pasteur. Mata Hari. Saint Lazarus gloriously resuscitated.

But they leave fearfully when the drum-roll is heard under the water.

Stage direction: Venice. The campanile, *la piazza de San Marco,* gondolas. The Parthenon, the Mona Lisa. The Leaning Tower. A Great Wall. One need not visit. Loplop, dumb with fear and fury, reclaims his boa and remains motionless for twelve days on both sides of the door.

The hundred headless woman and Loplop return to a savage state and cover the eyes of their faithful birds with fresh leaves. Max Ernst born in Brühl, 1891. Max Ernst discovers Mozart. Max Ernst survives the War. Max Ernst *dada.* Max Ernst *surrealisme.* Max Ernst accused. Max Ernst exonerated. Max Ernst goes to London. Max Ernst goes to New York. Max Ernst in Arizona. Max Ernst exhibits. I have not even begun to tell you about Max Ernst. This is intentional. The magician of barely detectable displacements, a swarm of bees in the palace of justice. Max Ernst dies.

The forest makes way for a united couple followed by a blind body.

(Loplop, the sympathetic demolisher and former Bird-Superior, fires a round of juniper berries at the debris of the universe. The hundred headless woman keeps her secret.)

WHO WAS SCHEHERAZADE

My job was to pick rocks. From his field. In lieu of rent. But the rocks were all limestone and were crawling with tiny fossils of various crustaceans & cephalopods & wavy ferny things that looked like plants to me but, on second thought, probably weren't, probably weren't plants at all but animals in the same way that a tomato is a fruit and not a vegetable.

I became distracted.

He would see me down in the lower field on his way from the house to the paddock and I would be staring raptly at a stone the size of my fist and he would call, "Everything OK?" And I would toss the stone into the wheelbarrow that rested ten, maybe twenty feet distant and I would call back "Yes. Everything's fine."

Sometimes I would enter the field late in the afternoon and find the wheelbarrow in place, a few small rocks already weighting its rusted udder. When I asked, he said "Oh, the children do that."

At the south edge of the pasture was a sinkhole that he used as a firepit. Trash from the house, trash lumber from his mill, anything he couldn't or wouldn't use. Once a month or so he burned off the sinkhole. The fires would burn for two or three days.

I was allowed to lob the rocks into the sinkhole if I wanted. Sometimes I did. Other times I took them in the wheelbarrow to the edge of the sinkhole and poured them in. Or I took them to the west edge of the field, where the erosion was bad, and filled the gullies.

Once I took a rock home. It had the most amazing fossils but was, like everything else, encrusted with manure & red clay. I scrubbed it, then left it in cold tap water for a week by my sink, then scrubbed it again. With a toothbrush.

I wondered whether the scrubbing, since it was limestone, would wear the fossils right off, so eventually I quit. Later I quit soaking it also.

Most days, when there was work, I worked at the cabinet shop on Hardinsburg Road. I ran the sander, stacked lumber, and generally kept up with the odd jobs. The cabinet shop was called Blue River Cabinetry, but the Blue River was actually some distance away. When I asked one of the owners about this, he shrugged and said, "It sounded nice."

Periodically a flash thunderstorm would wash through the pasture, deepening the sinkhole, eroding more of the west bank, and uncovering more rocks.

During the two months I lived there his wife did my laundry, on alternate Mondays. Once she got my underwear and his underwear confused. We thought we had it sorted out at the line but later I found that a few of his shorts & shirts had slipped into my drawers. I still have an undershirt of his that I wear, when it comes up in the pile.

WHAT IS SERIALISM

I'm afraid this is the film with the burning sheep in it. Again.

WHAT IS A KEY SIGNATURE

A collection of small items that could be mistaken for trees though not poplars maybe. A natural courtesy, a request for an orphanage. A salubrious assignation.

When many fixtures less the appearance of simplicity is brutal, a counterfeit dexterity. A stone is a plenary terminus, the extension of space past flesh counts as ample profile. A feeder moves more speedily.

A path a street a lane a court an alley a small road a winding stair.

WHAT IS A TENOR

If astonishment then replica. If porcelain than mourning. If hero then metamorphosis. If abstinence then flight.

Very well thank you. If yucca then savvy then delight.

WHAT IS A TRITONE

Volition. One begins then two then more than two, four, then five, is more than five a legitimate gratuity, ten, is twenty, is more than twenty.

One begins with a wound, is this what I'm hiding. To what extent does a wound express and is therefore audible, do guests at breakfast hear it, or as such, do they look up from a lingersome repast and do they then suggest therapy—a medical explanation—does this augment the estrangement, does it depend upon the number of guests.

Prohibited in some times and places. *Mi contra fa diabolus est in musica,* this was accepted wisdom, this is a syllabic conceit. In the garden where I walked. In the garden where I or anyone walked, where I heard, where anyone heard, where I called or was called and calling thus shifted the leaves from one green branch to another, I or anyone.

Is there more to come about food. Yes. In this poem. No.

A mendicant obsession, was this enough to cop a plea, to prompt a theft, when I first heard it I was in a spacious hall with poor acoustics in Cambridge, Massachusetts, it was a dusty place, though I was raised with a piano in the house, though I grew up singing I had not heard it before, I mean I had no name for it, can I or can anyone hear without taxonomy, can we name this tune. Machault Dufay Beethoven even John Cage if we so choose.

The wound does not heal. I pledge my kingdom but find only long sleep and a solo lament. This is established, this is recorded. This has already been committed to film.

Counterfeit coins in a leather purse.

By a pleasant fire one sits, one drinks, one can forget and if so does this make one separate, does one consent. By a pleasant fire the expulsion crouches in its liminal heat. Two long-stemmed yellow roses register the difference between precision and delight. Not hunger.

I am a guest, therefore am I wounded and do I hear it.

No weak broth, no superaltar; aspect's logical complaint. *I charge you, O ye daughters of Jerusalem.* One begins, two begin. One begins. One begins again.

WHAT IS A HEXACHORD

Blowing in from Matinicus from Criehaven this wind is a progressive advection, it lacks a consecutive dialectic, is this a hermitage, an unriddling, is it some new trick. Does a bridge cleanse and if so how will the children learn and when, how will they move. And be moved. To move. How will the children move and the wind as it brushes up past Boothbay into Booth Bay and into the river, when or how does a bay become a river or a river a bay, when I step into it, when I or anyone steps, when and what then is a child, did I carry or was I carried or is childhood really this daily island life.

If not why not.

But the wind blows. This is indisputable, this is the nature of wind, one does not have to be a bridge, to build a bridge, to negotiate a causeway to understand, one does not have to pledge one's self to alternative energy sources, it is enough to be a citizen, it is enough to learn. To be a citizen could mean to own a boat. It once meant this.

Low tide at Hodgdon Ledge. Is this a form of voting, have I performed my civic duty.

I have walked to the south pond and back and I have walked Long Cove on the east side and I have walked Long Cove on the west side. I have seen Tarbox Cove and Jewett Cove and Knubble Cove and Brooks Cove and I have walked on the East Shore Road and on the West Shore Road. I walk and have walked and in walking so walking do.

I sing as I walk when I have breath which is not always.

Have I tailored the sea-gale to any prior fallacy, have I discerned: the germ. The pattern. The sortilege, the apocalypse, the subliminal response.

To the traditional hexachords (hard/natural/soft) Guido d'Arezzo added the device known as the Guidonian Hand. Eleventh century. A physical mnemonic, as shin for sound or thumb for shoal. Gastrocnemius, the belly of the leg. *Ut re mi* now modernized in the movable-doh which some use which some do very well use but not so different not so very different no.

Oil sheen. If one makes a fetish of furniture can one travel there.

I score these words with my fingertips. Over the bay a lone tern is wheeling. There is not so much, not so much as I had thought, not much though it is enough, I thought, though I think, though I say, though I will never say it cannot be enough, I was once a child, it is enough to have been a child and to have known this, to know and to be, to ferry, to cross, to apprehend is to remember and it is enough, I know. And so the music makes me.

WHAT IS A BASS

For the months of the year go by gaily decked. January in her caramel shawl, February in her cranberry, March a sere presence. One by one as the Bayeux Tapestry endures. April in her citron, May in his green. With each thread a plan suggests that this is the most agreeable solution and fine indeed for a general leaving. June in his surfeit, July in her tallow shift. August not hardly. September September September who can imagine such a splendid petulance, who can gainsay the scope of his enquiry, who can indemnify, who might crown. October *idem.* As you have heard. And as we must now consider. November a lonely watch, smell of wet wool, a stone cairn at which one tarries and bequeaths. A glacial lake. Pure stream and pines.

December asks this of us and once no more.

WHAT IS A PIANO

Prophecy as in elucidate, prophecy as in foretell. A man with a vision in a mountain town can vet the difference: spruce this time. Cameras in risky places. The Sibyl in her cage, a dusty waltz, gram by gram as veneration limps earthward.

A prism inhabited by a small bird, a wren, maybe.

Bad parties are in evidence everywhere. Elementary school parties, blastocyst cotillions, tollkeeper jamborees. The worst parties. "Shuffleboard?" (Thank you, Mr. Bones.) *Le malheur indigène, la vierge vestal métaphysique.*

The more parties, the more rules for parties. Shanty-town meets sonnet-wallow.

I have been spying for a little over six hours now on the glass doorknob of the hairdresser at 6th & Clinton. The limbo provides a perfect post-colonial rubric.

One by one the accompanists, no longer needed, are dying from the boardwalks. They are incredibly soft in their last moments—like ripe gourds or velvet they are begging to be touched. They are nervous. No word has come from their advance scouts. They are fragile as soap bubbles, and as iridescent. They leave moist rings when they leave us.

Major media. An abduction that lies down at nightfall.

WHAT IS THE REAL ANSWER

There is this high keening I can do nothing about. It is the source of many things. The breaking of bread, for instance. A concealed (refr)action. There are small armies among us, and they seek out the most moist places.

Every sound is tropical, every sound is perishable. My aunt sends one wrapped in butcher paper & string. I refuse to open it and so it remains on a shelf next to Blackwell's *Curious Herbal* and a bag of homemade noodles, quivering.

In the eighteenth century it was not uncommon for large landowners to conclude that nursemaids were spies. *Dear outrageous cataleptic inhibitor,* their letters would begin, *Dear Anglophone gasconade.* Heft of a pomegranate.

I add cider vinegar, I add extra oil. Knead until the muscles of each palm register their pulsed exequies. The honey, the redress. The observer and the observed.

With maturity becomes the desire to be asked, no longer to play the supplicant. When my Lord asks a question winter answers for me. Why I prefer doors to windows, bridges to saints. Why insist on scumble.

(Do we choose the means of our drowning? Or do others choose for us?)

At night in my room I practice each dance step, slowly, carefully. After the manner of an exile.

In this dream I wash locks, tubs of Yales, until my fingers begin to bleed. I splash sudsy water on the cold flagstones. No one else is around. Every now and then I think I hear a sound from the next room, but I am mistaken.

WHAT IS PULSE

In the next apartment a telephone is ringing. I begin to count. After an interval it stops, and I think, *Someone has died.*

It begins to get colder. Tomorrow someone is coming to measure my radiators.

The beauty of war is the advancement of technology. Afterwards, new forms of entertainment arise in order to move product: Buffalo Bill's Wild West Show, General Electric, Mutual of Omaha. War is one long commercial for technology. We complain about it but secretly don't want it to end.

I think, *You are in China now.* I think, *You are searching for a flower that will correspond perfectly to the strawberry birthmark on your left hip.*

Colt, Remington, Peabody. The conveyance, the village, the self. In a free market economy the local is discounted like a polyester shift: it's there, but wrapped in plastic. Morton-Thiokol, Martin-Marietta. Nothing personal. At the subatomic level what we call movement is a convenient fiction.

Fresh from the funeral you wear scarlet leggings. I know this because I dreamt it, and then the temperature began to fall.

Some metals you heat to temper, some you cool. Napoleon advancing across Russia, thigh-deep in snow.

I think, *Theodore Roosevelt won a Nobel Peace Prize for negotiating an end to the Russo-Japanese conflict.* Old Rough 'n' Ready. He understood the difference between terminologies, between terms. It could be argued that he saved the buffalo. He understood conflict the way he liked a brisk walk around the Albany streets at evening. To work up the blood.

Colder yet. *You are striding now over a rough steppe.* High altitude, memories of the herd at St. Ignatius. And the chapel. A mass in your most holy name.

WHAT IS SFORZANDO

A new town, midsummer. Classical sidestreet allusions. A slur thrown, as from a car; unwanted pet. Soon to be feral.

O'Hara: "Art is not your life, it is someone else's."

A hollow to the voice: *breathe*. With training comes certain habits of mind, of body. A dark room. A conservatory conceit. And a faint memory of some stairs I was climbing. My nerves, trim dots and dashes. Taste, as for screwpine or sangria. One certain bliss.

When is volition a difference. *Mars Jupiter Spain* and some speak more distinctly, some are perfectly articulate. Each consonant less psalm than sparrow.

Any motion of the hand. In salute of what general. (I) dictate; dictator. And cession of anatomy in service of which song. Genuflection. Like that: holy.

Tropism of declare. Beethoven made much use of it.

The clenching to my palm makes a fist, the blossom of my fist wakes a wing. When a coulter withdraws from the body of a child what then is seen clearly. *If mine eye be darkened.* This, like flesh, for the licking. Surgical. Sweet. One of many diseases of the tongue.

WHAT IS A SOPRANO

I call to you as a prism to its oracle denies any prescriptive allure. What is a high sound when a sparrow takes it. When breath snatches. A latch catches. *Dear diary.* I am home now and affect a suitable disregard.

On a screen everyone is very particular. Does this explain.

It is this bird we want, not that one. This one not that one. Myth is the difference between birds.

Is this a letter for us to open. It is. Red yellow blue green and violet. Pressed between as petals in a bound volume for their proper keeping. Repeat, as necessary. A gift expresses the meek constituency of a recollected pleasure.

Who is happier when blind or blinded. Who says happy now.

WHAT IS AN ARPEGGIO

Men spaced evenly along a country lane. Bite of autumn. Desire a sharp thing, cold hung from its chainfall of sky and pierced lengthwise by small flocks of each breath. If any deer lives in mortal terror then is what I'm projecting an exercise in fidelity, is it any one-way street. A deer is a boundary, *deer* expresses space the way an artery separates *pulse* from *try*.

(Cold, and making clean love to horizon—a childhood. Can necessity have apprehended the persistence of grace, coterminous, while I stood with my back turned. While I shoplifted, while I prepared a meal on the old stove, while with one hand I rendered each tree porcelain. Still a finger: traces, each benison. Scraped thus I stand. With them or against them. A flail—)

Slow passage. Each pair of eyes turning. Under other circumstances I might say *hunger*.

A man walks into a bar, he is very chummy but also very thirsty, he prides himself in carrying correct change. By day he works as a foreman at the toll bridge—girders in the channel breeze, and the cranes, deepwater, lifting them out, one by one above the current's flow. He is dreaming even now of a shot that rings like a stolen bell, that he once stole, or should have stolen, a bell he could yet steal—he imagines—(though he will not)—the shot rings like that, and once only, and he feels the chill and so he says to the bartender—

(Or, one could argue sympathy is just a cheap trick. An egg with a double yolk, or with the embryo inside, clot of blood and the rest a dull flake, resistant. A hungry man will have eggs with his bacon, grits with his eggs, he will be sure of his hunger, it is a tune he whistles often because like any boundary the sea remains with us, water and salt as in the body of that which crosses, flared and flaring. Faint scent of graphite and musk that means *man,* to say the cold cuts "like a knife" is to minimize the complicity of the vertical, the immensity of scale. I open my mouth and something small & warm escapes. An oak leaf like a brown hand flattened wet against the denim of my calf, I stroke each rib to find out what's missing—)

It is good to be sure of at least one thing lest the world prove weightless. One hoof strikes pavement, *someone raises a gun.* It could be me. I could be blind.

WHAT IS A CANTILENA

I was introduced to a child and I asked him how old he was, that is, how much of a child he was, to what extent he was a child, to what extent he had left of childhood and to what extent he felt this, did he feel it, was this merely an ordinal concern. He answered, "Five."

And so I asked him when he would turn six, by which I meant how much is five from six, should I or should anyone take into account the minutely fractional value of time, what then is the relationship between quantum mechanics and identity or in the evolving notions of self, the construction of innocence, what then is innocence, innocence is an oil painting, innocence is any landscape covered in fresh snow, it is a mathematical conceit, this is axiomatic, any child knows this as it knows any child, this is why a child as a child (that is *child* qua *child*) (even this child, this particular child) cannot know innocence, because innocence is external to childhood, it is discrete, it is extraneous, it is vertical, it is literally out of bounds.

Eventually the borders of childhood are enlarged; innocence obtrudes. We call this *adulthood.*

So I asked him when he would turn six, and he looked at me, and blinked, and said, "When I'm done being five."

And we walked out into the snow together, because it was Maine and it was winter, and there was a great deal of snow, old snow and new snow, and he sniffled because he had a cold though when I asked him he said he felt fine, and I asked was he sure, and he said well no he didn't really feel very good, so I asked if he wanted to go back inside but he said no, he wanted to be outside, that was what he really wanted, and I understood, because that was what I wanted too, to be outside, only for me there was no more outside, as such, there was only snow, as there was only Maine,

38

in winter, and I took his hand, because we were going to cross a busy road, and we did, and on the other side there was more snow, and a dark school, and stars above, the air was very crisp and silent and we walked slowly, because he was not yet done with being five, and because I was, and so we walked slowly, along a busy road, and I wanted to make a painting of it, or an equation, but I did not know how.

WHAT IS COUNTERPOINT

The study of a near fear which effects architecture, as floor to door, as door to floor, as floor to more and in an advanced state portico, cupola, balustrade, dormer. Subtended without benefit of a sublime elevation.

In aeternam. In New Mexico a miracle, in New Mexico the mere fact of red is a singular indulgence. As such wary.

A steep reluctance beyond which no pain passes. Yet dwells there.

Every day the advocacy of a standard tone, solfege of distance and dancing. And as act of faith rendered logical, that is visible, this is not difficult, this is merely placement and voice. Redacted for posterior semblance.

How much means one touch.

When I walked out this morning when I walked out when I walk when I was I was out walking. An orchid. In shade. In shade made and played.

WHAT IS A DESCANT

An apple in December. Sweet. Will ask upwards. Will move from side to side as if a great earthwork nudging past attraction into some valid spectrum. Sweet. Will recede from this frame coupled by portrait and with fresh nefarious but not often. Sweet. Will approach a singular grief, subsume a guileless endeavor. Sweet. Sweet. Will not fall.

WHO IS JOHANNES OCKEGHEM

The poets of the West repeat their names for things—flora, fauna, topography —ceaselessly, as if to charm back the real. The same way you & I sometimes, mistakenly, insert a "the" in front of *Hagia Sophia.*

Today: a small length of string, any blade for cutting. I take a smooth cheese from the cupboard and begin to slice it. Wanting to convince myself.

The poets of the West are attuned to the iconography of specie. Fauna to cravat, figured headdress to domed memorial. This is chump change; we all know it. A broken abacus in an island nation.

May I redirect your attention from the pale hand reaching over the low stone wall to the impeccable sunset. From Native to native. We have, with the help of the Irish and the Poles, survived something inward.

There is gravity, and then there is history. Constantinople, for example. Reading red for "read," white for "white." And not relying, merely exposed vein, the rope of it a tree the hand makes when held to dazzle—

The poets of the West agree: in the opera, Pirandello is a stand-in for Pirandello. (And the cold expression of the chest, to govern.)

The poets of the West dream of Jeffers in his tower by the sea.

WHAT IS CADENCE (I)

I was not alone, I had neither fallen nor scraped the recourse of any thoughtless benevolence from the rubber heel of my good shoe, I was a precise emancipation. Tryst of yarrow. It was spring.

By sinking the transverse roads Frederick Law Olmsted sought to prevent the twentieth century. Passing the Pioneers Gate a young girl points, cries *Park, park!*

Imagine an old-style hunting horn, spiralled and flared, once voluble but spackled now in directive disregard. Turn here, *sign here.* (My heavenly postman.) Were I to wrap this in what length and then too the arraignment, imputation of complicity, the lovers tender in their smocked shifts.

Consider Lydia: harvest of murex, specie passing through dyed hands each day at market, invoice a like liege and no less clever yet.

Breastbone and contact. Is this loyalty, is this an object of ultimate concern.

And the remainder, perfervid offscouring, mere pendulum husk: forty elements within an oak's breadth of battered glass. I SPY. *Phrygian:* I should not have felt this way. *Authentic:* I should not have come.

WHO IS ANTON WEBERN

The stars excluded. Asperged their absences begin to make common cause. Epode of dress: cum filial introspection there exists no more perfect theft than a sensible relict. Bed/spread. Commingling at the sill of a dry fountain we begin to sing in low sorrel tones.

In this niche a man, a cell, a desk, a tablet. In the next, *idem.*

Another chapter in the dialectic between dust & key. Steel sliver to keep the elements out: barium, fabularium, sodium pentathol. Climate of axon. This explains: whist, pinochle, rook. This does not explain: ____ _____.

In Lovingston, Virginia, six acres appreciate in inverse proportion to the latest & most visible orogeny. We want to believe in the Commune, we want to believe in the dead.

Exoticism as windfall. We send in a reporter, she shoots rolls of film, we promote and later suppress any resulting images: ablute serial malfeasance. Overhead the sky is a blank form awaiting Balzac's signature.

An arcature of keys, diminishing rapidly. A leather harness.

Risk of immobility in the night passage. Hagar & Tamar, shirred vanish of Gatling.

Poker, roulette, the invention of plate glass. At some speeds an image. Inverted: as retinal value, happy accident! The split quill recoils. And 'struths on. Nothing to start with / a general swelling of the cranium.

A patriotic medley may be played. Cable access. Two farmers, tired, crossing an old field at dusk. A third raddle: (s)he who waits

[motion for water from the furthest cell]

WHAT IS A CITTERN

Body of rose lie down at daybreak, ebony shadow, duplication of breathe. My voice is not essential. When a rotary covenant is unavailable the incarceration cinches, garment as from the late woolen centers of the deciduous plain.

(A group of INMATES sandblasts the east exterior wall of the Shrine to Music.)

Figuration of the neck, three heads—two human—armigerous. As for fray, for vitrine. What issues. An identity: a Maltese cross, a game of chess.

In a high place many men in rough tunics lie bleeding. Runnel of flagstone, litmus: legend. We pretend indifference. The ivory hairpin, the secreted cameo—all govern. *Step onto the mixolydian scale.*

As carved from a single block of wood. Head, neck, soundboard.

Open scrollwork: hieroglyphic of a nervous recompense. If one could stop one's ears. And see, simply. As bolt from blow. The hand in its "cheerful" pantomime: blood-fat, like a sausage. Touching here & (now) here. We surmise. Imbrication of chalcedony.

Still the wave seeks, beneath muslin, through closed doors. If a hand strikes a chord and no lover hears it, does the forest advance?

For no sedimentary pleasure. Deeply worn frets.

One always suspects the forest but the forest is not always there. Cowslip & nettle: (breeding place for): wyvern, broken consort. As though *come shrieking down from the night sky, twig of thyme left rustling—*

(The INMATES collect their tools, turn the corner of the building. They are laughing lightly, comfortably as they walk away.)

WHO IS FRIEDRICH VON SCHILLER

Sweet Clio deals: six of Darwin, ratchet of Marx. Outside a lone eagle circles the river's frozen cuff. Memories of Jarts, advancements in the mechanical production of flour. A pharmacological solution. Spotlit ruins parkside.

If jewelry then closet. Peristyle of ruby: who dwells there. Pure circuitry of the modern toaster threads this needle. Sire of a malingering architecture / as drop cloth, as putty.

Design of a traditional Hopi clay oven. "As though one could walk there." Figure of a thrush in the Tower of London.

The next divination will be a single beggar. Either he wants a story or he is a story. A thin crust. Crepitant master of phenobarbitol. A tortoise stalks as slowly: time leas(h)ed.

A theory of prey: *We're all looking for a foothold outside negligence.* Hence viscera, haruspexy. The media is the massage. As lentils from cinder. Metrical device as placeholder, a sincere involvement that renders one more "sleeper" than (s)he already is.

Boredom as physical sensation vs. boredom as psychosocial pathology. A brooch the shape of a human tongue, cast in gold. Sacramental renunciation—image for image—blooded on both cheeks after the first kill.

"You think you are going to enjoy kissing your girlfriend, but then you hate it." Groucho & the stockbrokers. Opposed: afterglow of the Byronic hero.

In the ancient kingdom of Arrhythmia the person of the deity was conceived to be bipartite, shaft vs. fletch, pulse vs. caesura. A capricious god. Nightly the cakes of dull flaxseed. Elmflicker. Ashtigmatism. Cerements in the garish of the banefire: we are all (br)others now.

WHAT IS AN ARPANETTA

No false Pevensie will enter. Boyhood, obsession with medieval weaponry as with poisons. The body to be kept intact. Blunt objects. Or, the dart's flecked puncture: agency deferred. Scant vector of aluminum in a prairie town.

Curdle of old coffee in the well of a shoulderblade.

Somewhere in Alsace the former manufactory of bell-pulls. Birdlime etc. Grandchildren of the last craftsmen wander the square, opening & closing their hands experimentally. Every now & then one lets loose a cry of frustration, or delight.

Sardine of the breath, phoretic flicker. From the bandstand click of a heel like a tooth. Andiron of the rough trade: less useful in the singular. Hospital reached through a smudged mirror in the rue de Superiour.

At the dispensary the agent issues small slips of thin, brightly-colored paper. And leans low, and whispers.

Iridescence of grackle. No remedial heat access.

Up the flue: all evidence of dance. Cut glass of the decanter, stray taffeta from the hardwood floor. To pluck (crow quills) ((as harpsichord)) vs. to strike (leather-covered mallets). We search the smoke for signs.

WHAT IS ICTUS

A clean sweep. A dark sleep. When does sheen inhabit a physical discourse, I mean this soft blending. Blue plinth rasp. One. One. One.

WHAT IS BALLET

A small pebble at the bottom of a swift clear stream. Or, several.

WHAT IS AN ALTO

Classicism.

(The underworld subsists on a bedrock introspection otherwise known as time. Into this frame obtrudes consciousness also a superior penury. Not a fresh agon, unhousing and unhoused, not unlike a similar ploy. Virescent. Stained with salt. Some brushed bower seen.)

WHAT IS SELAH (II)

Gyroscope and speculum. Anyone's fireside angel. My actuarial zeal.

WHAT IS A HORNPIPE

(But when she called to me it was always *Mr. Monroe Doctrine, Mr. Monroe Doctrine.* I wanted to seize the moment very badly but the best I could do was Brazil. That, or plastic surgery. Or else my ragtime in cold cash. She crossed her arms: *Wrong century!* Ka-ching. I was devastated. She set a bonfire for my ruffles & jabots. All the small countries attended, even a few that weren't really countries yet but had set up embassies in hope. It was hard to tell their flags from the flames, at least until I realized that some of their flags *were* flames. *That's right,* I thought, but said nothing aloud. By then she was busy with her welder's hood and her gemstones. I sauntered over to the concession booth and ordered an Ashoka Pillar with a side of fries. Looking back, that's what I regret most about those years: the philatelophagy. I was sending messages to all my most elementary particles. Sometimes they would tap back, as if welded into a steel hull. Doomed semaphore! Can a part haunt the whole? I was absurdly coifed. All my friends were working for Parker Brothers. In the end I sold my collection of antique thuribles, no longer having any shelves to store them. She'd say *Jump.* I'd say *How sly.*)

WHAT IS THE BROTHERHOOD

Nobody is at home here. In my small room: cot, writing desk, rickety chair. A basket containing an apple and a few cookies wrapped in a cloth napkin. A note: *Lavatory down your hall to the left!* I feel I am here to be cured of something. Outside: ranks of young men in blazers, walking their mastiffs. A stiff March breeze.

The mistress invites me to meals. While she finishes the cooking, I draw toys from a large wooden box, show each to her son. He is five but does not yet talk. He watches intensely. I show him: a miniature circus, carved from boxwood & purpleheart; he shakes his head no. A plastic green hippo: no. An alabaster yo-yo on a bright crimson thread: no.

I give up. My hands fall empty into my lap. Suddenly he nods: *That's it, that's it exactly.* His mother steps swiftly from the stove, pulls him to her: "Don't encourage him."

(Later, he draws a picture with crayons. A black hat, unblinking spectacles, nothing else but lots of blue-grey hatchwork. Printed crookedly across the bottom: G.C. IN FOG.)

10 o'clock. Those who have other duties leave the hangar. Those who make toys for a living remain where they are.

I have been issued a power drill. My job is to screw black wooden knobs to the toy appliances as they come down the line. And plastic cups to the sand tables.

Over the loudspeaker: "The Feuerbach convoy is approaching the east gate." With the rest I am hustled out into the dooryard, in view of the road. I blink against the midday sun. One of the women is frantically arranging us in rows: tall, short, kneeling down front. *"Smile,"* someone hisses.

I sweep the flagstones beneath the almond trees. I have no dustpan and am unsure whether using one's fingers is permitted. For a minute or two I stand, uncertain. Then I use the broom very carefully to spread the blossoms, dust, & dead leaves back evenly over the courtyard.

The master wishes to see me. We sit on a low bench outside the cobbler's shop. (I keep furtively checking my shoes.) He asks me if I know how to quarter an apple. I say I do. He looks at me for a moment with an expression that could be suspicion or disappointment.

During dinner the walls are surrounded by a ring of former inhabitants. They sing songs, but our songs are louder. They carry placards in a language I can't read. After a while they go away. Later I find a note one of them dropped: *doz. Eggs. Cleanser. Dye packets. —Snow?*

APOSTROPHE TO THE MEMORY
OF BENJAMIN BRITTEN

I shall now speak about kittens.

The quality of kittens is not strained. The quality of kittens is not stained. So be it. O live hive, O you of the dancing paw. In the flank of the bookcase a visible flaw, the pit of an olive, the tip of a live oak, *I saw in Mississippi a live-oak growing* and in its branches kittens, no among its roots kittens, that is right, that is proper, that is more agreeable to the bees who in fact attest, arrest the branches, who tie the branches to the trunk with their gold thread. O you of the dancing flaw, O yew of the 'mancing claw, O hedge matted by fog until it becomes (has become) a private thing, a picklock, a password, O contraband dynamo. If I am approached by youth and step back then what. *Somewhat afear'd* said the old sailor. A weaning and not more than that specific saucer of fresh milk, *For I believe lately I think of little else than of them. Yet it remains* to speak more freely of the device of the parenthesis. Raised to commerce a word nevertheless knows to track small motion as lizards of the desert know just when to drop their grails. I mean tails. Harvested & sewn into coats of great value *without a friend or lover nearer* than this house of sticks. O cultivator of cravats, O splendid warp from wolf suspended, O mercy of the barre.

Go wicked wicket into the wide wide world.

Speaking about kittens concluded.

WHAT IS RADIO

A talking like the bark of a tall tree. And we approach and we do feel it,
we are in agreement on the duress that leads up from pavement across
parched grass and toward the vertical, this is a natural progression and
so very fine

for discourse, any serviceable discourse will do, any hierarchy, styptic
impulse—

We consent. And call this *swarm,* as with bees in a hive, we are confused
as to the agent but at least the gesture is clear: aloft: desiring: the sigillary
mark, this is the ecstasy of the language

and passing through as we pass (through) we feel nothing as the tree
feels (nothing), as we run hands abreast: its length, rough or smooth: let
us assume it is a hemlock, let us assume it is a yew, let us assume these
hands

as we assume once more the dark garb of the stereopticon, the
aspergillum, one static motion

because there is a third cell in the eye that witnesses to the light

in the same way the Witnesses come, in twos to residence with their
gaudy palettes, their magentas and teals. We open a door and there stand
they as the cells of each eye: open, innocent of prejudice: innocent of
sight even, microscopic. The body clocks brightness the way emptiness
cues gravity

but we were speaking of speaking, that delirious amplitude. The kiss.
A handshake: misnomer, elision of the plural. *For it must needs be that
offences come; but woe to that man by whom the offence cometh,*

tubules of bergamot fringing a mountain meadow. Glycerine, a finer toss. Hobnail of chimney. The world runs upward in a great pall. What quays horizontal s(t)aves us.

WHAT IS A CANZONE

Geneva as a system: of stoppages, exquisite needlework, of the catalogue of the Prinzhorn Collection. A venerable casuistry. Yet dwells there. May line its nest with stray objects / some shiny, some soft. In the nature of lay.

East of Mishawaka the country opens into itself like snowfall. Thumb-check & broomstraw, baby's breath, lily of the valley. Prayer comes to seem like just another bleak exercise in consensual harbor abuse.

There is another story, the story of Science and of the fierce breath of Science. The pocket drone, the soul cured of its grey animal.

FORTRAN as a provisional malady, neoclassical representations of the ideal city. In exile the clouds seem larger, more outlandish.

Aside from mitosis no one's getting any younger here. Cab Seven to Base: "Should I pick up the blood then?" Base: "Yes." Cab Seven: "So call ahead. You know I hate to wait." Base: "You know you always have to wait."

WHAT IS A HEMIOLA

I send you this Ingram, this tangram, this dancegram—O fortunate swash-buckler! In the afterglow of midhusbandry indelible fractions hover.

WHAT IS A THRENODY

Abscissa of value, technochrome. This ceaseless (re)vision.

If she were then would she have a name. Thus plum, thus poplar, thus obelisk through which a faint cleansing as with grit from the soft palette. Foraging in the nerve bolus.

A sample lens, a stippled bone. Pin to penitent. With diligent stress on a flat table or slight palm of a seaside town.

Some countries of the world exist now only in the form of obsolete postage, as angels or capitals. This is considered perfectly normal. We call a hole a grave if we value what goes into it, a mine if we value what comes out.

The instrument at hand. (The instrument. The hand.)

No snide experiment. A broken filament like a pearl must be drawn from the lip of a bruised music.

Bus stop, box step. Dark Goshen prey.

WHAT IS A MOTET

Acquired: abstract reasoning. Through a series of correspondences (cup from crayon, table from plate) what portion of the visible readership remained gathered in that room.

The poets of that place all had gills. They swerved like daisies on the hillsides of memory: a sort of promissory trope. Bergomask & denticle. I asked for the secrets of the vaulted sky but in lieu of answer they waved brightly-colored handcloths in the spring breeze.

In a plague year any city visits fable nationally, this is not intentional, this is the outcome of a viviparous satiation.

A folksinger stands in a garden. A boy presents a duck to his mother. Wind fishes the ice-pond for its winter hair.

If a bound volume adduces the status of a more fearful insufflation then without damage can it be sewn. Tallis or Byrd or Byrd or Tallis. Tallis or Byrd or Byrd or Tallis. Can one compliment, can one vary, can one see both ways. Yes lightly and yes nightly. Yes brightly. Yes nimbly and so.

WHAT IS A BALLAD

The moon's guitar is a precious instrument we yearn for with the heart of a tunnel in the cloth & leather rucksack of the night.

WHO IS THELONIOUS MONK

Misery labors under a sabine enchantment. She shakes her copper locks; they rattle as the ships pass through, one by one. Smaller vessels portage. Potash, scrimshaw, bicarbonate of soda. No willpower need apply.

WHO IS STEVE REICH

EVERY. GOOD. BOY. DOES. FINE.

WHAT IS AN ORATORIO

Throne. Foil. Joist. Timbrel. Indent. Vine. Advection. Hook. Reply.

WHAT IS ACCIACCATURA

(This is not about you. Understand. This is not, this has never been about you.)

WHO WERE THE LORELEI

The question of whether what the sea brings to our feet is "artificial" or not. As in touched by the hand, as in hand-made. This tide of mussels.

We walk up the draw at a steady pace. If I say "words keep us warm" then you know I am lying, you pull your sweater tighter, your dog lunges at her leash.

At the apex it seems likewise appropriate to communicate, if not to one another, then to another. Technology vs. possession. *Verso*, hunger; *verso*, lack of paperwork translating badly into static, then silence.

There is never any cognizance in the repatriation. I give back and this seems like the most natural & appropriate gesture.

The idea that two figures cast three shadows is an old one, persuasive in some cultures. I point out the tunneling, over & over again: entrances & exits. Nothing is what it appears to be, I say. To which you reply, *yes it is.*

WHAT IS A METAPHOR

A humorous joke at the expense of this month's endangered species. Walking by the lagoon it seems improbable: that we laugh? That we remain silent? That we walk at all? Mud clinging to the reeds which cling in turn to the cuffs of our pants which are not actually ours: proximity vs. resistance.

A colonial language which becomes the official language of the post-colonial state which becomes the price of admission into the metropolis.

Onward Christian soldiers. When I was a child the Baptists stood up when the accompanist pounded the opening chords of "Stand Up, Stand Up for Jesus," but the Methodists remained seated. This was a neater division than class, one we pleated every summer in the orchard between the roots of the damsons.

Asphalt poured over disturbed ground—it appears solid, but it's not.

An admission of doubt, which is not the same thing as an admission of guilt but will suffice in most kitchen recipes. Our own traces, for example: in June dust. In June dusk. At the length of its tether desire comes bounding back. A whistle will do it. The right word, spoken in an even, conversational tone. Though it brings a death. The crust shot through with its leaven.

Boys, dikes, wooden shoes. Vast sibling rivalry. A lisp affected in criminal court. Someone or something has been burning.

WHAT IS PERFORMANCE

I implore clarity one last time. No noose replies. Sinuous furlongs of ocean light chitter one to another in the livid estuary. Correlatives sink. Flensed bodies of seals sink faster, into sand. Think of the gulls as morticians.

A small card encountered at a bookstore, crimson upon crimson so that the card itself appears blank except for color, the skin of it.

Row houses, hunched up in that place like a New England far from home, that is, bigger than they should be. Sterile. As salt spray. And like moniker no firmer. Residual bay voltage. A flotilla of creosote.

Six wooden spools when last I checked. Slow pumice shortage. *Double agent!* Selling a daughter's school collages at a yard sale.

To be approached by the beast. And let us say the beast is hungry. And let us say the beast is rabid. And let us say the beast is blind—

WHAT IS A TESTIMONY

Brocade of the frozen lake. Diaspora of shore ice, just waiting, wait: the boys with their skates will come, will come with their skates, will come skating. Putting on & taking off. As if there were no difference. Waiting, and wait, the weight of it

As in simple, as in mercy. The quality of which may or may not, as the ice on the lake may be: strained: by temperature, by pressure of the water, by the pressure of that which walks. By the drills of the ice fishermen. By the cutter in the channel. Each with its agenda, each winter's addenda

Without which, say, spring would not → come. (If a tree falls. If the first fragment of ice detaches, slips into and then finally beneath the current, and no one is there. To see. If

I were to step out onto the ice. And keep walking. Or skating. (Though I have no skates. It's OK for me to tell you that, now. Though I have never. Told another. So: let us say

Walking. In shoes that slip on the ice. In shoes that just keep slipping. Not made → for this. They know I am going somewhere, these shoes, it is part of their duty to apprehend the artifice of motion, though not the nature or identity of destination. No holt, no heaven. And not happy about that. Shoes are seldom narrative creatures and yet they exist, ideally, in

Pairs and laced: their(s) (a) bondage. As with ice, cinch of ice on the lake, above the current, its darker darkness, straitening of small life. Who would keep going, what fool so late in winter. In love with the ice, with the idea of

(If a tree falls. Nor was I. As you were not. No one to bring back report. And the ice held for another month, in that time and in that place. And no one was lost to the water. And yes. I was lonely. We gave thanks.)))

Note

Archicembalo is structured after the fashion of a *gamut,* or musical self-instruction primer that often prefaced volumes of 19th-century American sheet music.

In musicological terms, *gamut* originally meant the note G at the pitch now indicated by the lowest line of the traditional bass staff. The Greek character gamma was used for its designation, and as this note just happened to be the *ut* (or *doh*) of the lowest notatable hexachord, "gamut" was adopted as an appropriate descriptor (gamma-ut).

Later, the word was used as a comprehensive label for the whole series of hexachords as displayed in musical scores. By further extension it came to mean any musical scale, and eventually the whole range of musical sounds, from lowest to highest. It was also, of course, applied metaphorically to a singer or actor's range, as in the colloquial phrase "to cover (or run) the gamut."

Somehow the word also came to designate the self-instruction primers early American publishers often used to preface bound volumes of sheet music. "The Gamut, or Rudiments of Music"—as it appeared in such important 19th-century folk repositories as *The Southern Harmony* and *The Sacred Harp*—was typically structured in a question-and-answer, or call-and-response fashion, as a dialogue between a teacher and a student. The gamut in the 1854 edition of *The Southern Harmony* begins

> PUPIL. What is music?
> TEACHER. Music is a succession of pleasing sounds.

and continues through the vocal parts, musical scales, rhythm, time signatures, basic musical notation, a smattering of music theory, and even a few remarks on conducting and performance practice.

The word *archicembalo* was first used in 1555 by Nicola Vicentino to designate a harpsichord equipped with many divided keys, or even a second manual, in order to permit the playing of his reconstructions of the diatonic, chromatic, and enharmonic scales of the ancient Greeks. Later writers applied the term to any enharmonic keyboard equipped for playing microtonal music. Such keyboards flourished during the 16th and 17th centuries and are known with anywhere from 24 to 60 keys per octave (Vicentino's had 35). The playing and tuning of such instruments has always been extremely difficult, and typically relegated to experimental quarters, at least prior to the rise of more general interest in microtonal music in the twentieth century.

Sources: *The Concise Oxford Dictionary of Music* (4th ed.); the *Grove Dictionary of Music and Musicians* (online ed.); *The Southern Harmony and Musical Companion* (1854 ed., repr. University Press of Kentucky, 1987).

Acknowledgments

Many thanks to the editors of the publications in which these poems first appeared, a few in earlier versions:

Antioch Review: "What is a Bass"
Aufgabe: "What is an Alto," "What is a Soprano," "What is Ictus," "What is Ballet," "What did Julius Steinberg," "What is Selah" (II), "What is Counterpoint," "Who were Noriko & Coahminan"
Colorado Review: "What is Sforzando," "Apostrophe to the Memory of Benjamin Britten"
Conduit: "What is a Testimony," "What is a Motet"
Conjunctions (web version): "What is Cadence" (II), "What is a Tritone," "What is a Hexachord," "What is a Piano," "What is Pulse," "What is the Real Answer"
Copper Nickel: "Who is Johannes Ockegehm," "Who are Gilbert & Sullivan" (I & II), "What is Performance"
Court Green: "Hymn Trick," "Who is Hildegard von Bingen," "Who were the Lorelei"
Denver Quarterly: "What is an Arpeggio," "What is Radio," "What is a Cantilena," "Who is Anton Webern"
Diode: "What is an Antiphon," "What is a Hemiola," "What is a Mordent," "What is an Oratorio," "What is an Overtone," "What is Belcanto," "What is Serialism," "What is a Tenor"
Double Room: "What is Tempo," "Who is Frei Manuel Cardoso"
Greatcoat: "What is a Descant," "What is a Threnody"
Hambone: "What is Opera," "Who is Josquin des Prez," "Who is Friedrich von Schiller," "What is an Arpanetta," "What is the Brotherhood"
Harp & Altar: "What is a Canzone," "What is a Cittern"
The Hat: "A Short History of Gorse"
New American Writing: "What is an Anthem," "Who is Charles Ives," "What is Cadence" (I), "What is a Hornpipe," "What is a Metaphor"
Octopus: "Who is Carl Stalling," "What is a Hymn," "What is Melisma," "What is a Symphony," "Who are the Other Gods"
Pleiades: "Who was Scheherazade"
Pool: "What is a Key Signature," "What is a Fugue"
Salt Hill: "What is a Selah" (I), "What is a Gimel," "What is a Mensuration Canon"
XConnect: "What is a Zither"

"What is a Hexachord" also appeared in *PP/FF: An Anthology,* ed. Peter Conners (Starcherone Press, 2006). "What is a Hymn" and "What is Selah" (I) appeared in *Joyful Noise: An Anthology of American Spiritual Poetry,* ed. Robert Strong (Autumn House Press, 2006). "Who is Josquin des Prez" is scheduled to appear in *An Introduction to the Prose Poem,* ed. Brian Clements (Firewheel Editions, 2009). This manuscript won the 2006 Alice Fay Di Castagnola Award from the Poetry Society of America, judged by Forrest Gander.

Several poems also appeared in *Arrangements for Halocline and Orchestra,* a limited-edition artist's book by printmaker Greg Murr.

"What is Opera" collages from the text of Max Ernst's *La femme 100 têtes,* transl. Dorothea Tanning (New York: George Braziller, 1981). "Apostrophe to the Memory of Benjamin Britten" quotes from Whitman's "I Saw in Louisiana a Live-Oak Growing."

Thanks to the Robert M. MacNamara Foundation and the MacDowell Colony, to my parents, and to Tony Farrington, Ilya Kaminsky, Brigit Kelly, Paul McCormick, Cole Swensen, Arthur Sze, and Rosmarie Waldrop. Special thanks to the National Music Museum in Vermillion, South Dakota, where the arpanetta, Julius Steinberg's saxophone, and the cittern in question—along with many other wondrous objects, from fipple flute to theremin—reside.